AF606911

My Life is a Poem About Flying Pigs

My Life is a Poem About Flying Pigs

Bruce M. Stachenfeld

Prospecta Press

Paperback ISBN 978-1-63226-176-2
Hardcover ISBN 978-1-63226-177-9

Published by
Prospecta Press
PO Box 3131
Westport, CT 06880

www.prospectapress.com

Book and cover design by Alexia Garaventa

This book is dedicated to the following people:

To my family and my friends. Being with you has been the spice of my life, and many of my poems derive from our time together. Thank you for being with me—both in good times and not-so-good times. You have given me the strength to keep trying to do impossible things.

To my wife, Ann, aka Sweetie Pig. You have always been a Flying Pig to me.

Life is poetry, if you let it be that way.

As I thought about a title for this book, I reflected that the most meaningful part of my life has been trying to do things, and think about things that seem impossible—like Flying Pigs.

This book contains varied poems from my life experiences, but a consistency is that many of the poems revolve around my acting and thinking in this way—hence the title.

Also, for reasons that have never quite been determined, love of pigs has become a defining characteristic for my wife and me. More on that below.

I hope when you read this book that you will enjoy the poems, and that they will inspire you to believe in your own Flying Pigs.

A BIT ABOUT THE AUTHOR

Bruce likes to write "to make the world a better place," and he hopes that these poems will have that effect. He has written extensively with this goal in mind, mostly in the genre of how-to books. Books so far include:

- A best-selling book on sales and marketing, designed to help those struggling to succeed in this difficult and often heartbreaking field—*If You Want to Get Rich, Build a Power Niche*;
- *The Real Estate Philosopher's Guide*, published under the pseudonym of the title, a compendium of articles Bruce has written over a decade, all intended to inspire outside-the-box-thinking to players in the real estate industry;
- With David Dowell as co-author, *How to Invest in Commercial Real Estate if You Know Nothing About Real Estate*, designed to prevent novice real estate investors from being taken to the proverbial cleaners in their early real estate investments.

More books with the theme of Making the World a Better Place are in the queue, including *Confessions of a Workaholic*, to help and guide those in the thralls of workaholism, and a treatise on *How to be a Good Man*. And yes, all of these are passion projects, i.e. Flying Pigs, for Bruce.

Bruce's poetry has the same purpose, and as a derivation of his life experiences, the poems enable the reader to learn from Bruce's (many) mistakes and at the same time be inspired by his successes.

In his other life, Bruce is one of the most well-known names in the real estate industry, from his founding of one of the top real estate law firms in New York City, Adler & Stachenfeld, LLP, to becoming a thought leader through a widely disseminated blog under his pseudonym *The Real Estate Philosopher*.

Bruce has also written fiction under his pseudonym James T. Hogg, and his first novel, *Faythe of North Hinkapee*, is an award-winning epic historical novel story set in Colonial times, with an indomitable female protagonist who seeks vengeance against the powerful family whose sons attacked her sister. A sequel is in the works.

Bruce is in his mid-sixties now, but he will tell you he has the energy of a twenty-year-old and is just getting started. Bruce loves that guy you might have seen in the Dos Equis beer commercials, who supposedly said, "The Most Interesting Man's one regret is not knowing what regret feels like."

Bruce wants that to be his only regret, too. So he has launched **The Bruce Projects** (www.thebruceprojects.com), pursuant to which he now just tries to say yes to every possible thing that he has never done before, and then see what happens. So far this has included writing philosophical dialogs, taking singing lessons, trying stand-up comedy (and learning the hard way why they call flopping "dying out there"), going on a safari to Africa, collecting several hundred bottles of scotch, collecting decorative pigs (a lot of pigs) with his wife, and taking up smoking (just a few) cigars.

Bruce lives in New Jersey with Ann, his wife of forty years, whom he is utterly crazy about. He does his writing at his beach house named Hogg's House, in Cape May, New Jersey. He has two grown daughters he is immensely proud of.

As noted above, pigs have become a defining characteristic for Bruce and Ann, who is now known affectionately as Sweetie Pig. Together they have put pigs everywhere, including their house in New Jersey that some call: *The Pig House.* The name is well-deserved since the house has well over 1000 pigs in it plus eleven pig topiaries in the front yard. Bruce and Ann throw ritual Pig Parties (roughly every three years), which include hog-calling contests, live pigs and, most recently, a performance of *The Pigoletto*, written by Bruce, which is an operatic version of *The Three Little Pigs* (available for viewing on **The Bruce Projects** website mentioned above).

Together, Ann and Bruce started The Sweetie Pig Foundation to "spread joy and happiness in the world." It is no coincidence that the logo for The Sweetie Pig Foundation is, yes, a flying pig.

One of Bruce's goals, which is not yet achieved, is to have a live pig as a pet; however that is where his wife has drawn a line in the sand. Her view is that there is a limit, but Bruce keeps hoping that she will change her mind.

Bruce is most proud of having successfully competed in two Ironman races, including the championship race in Kona, Hawaii. More recently, he pulled off a fitness initiative that he called "Ripped at 65," despite having open-heart surgery during his sixty-fifth year.

Finally, Bruce has loved living his life and this book is a collection of poems, reflecting his experiences, insights and continuing attempts to make pigs fly.

INTRODUCTION

My name is Bruce, and I fell in love with poetry about ten years ago.

Over the years I found myself writing poems on trains, in cars, in bars, parks, and even in bathrooms, dare I say.

When a thought hits me that is poem-worthy, I scribble it down and sometimes over a year later it evolves into a poem.

At first it was just fun, but then it started to blossom as I found that when I read the poems to people they seemed to enjoy them. Go figure that.

This resulted in my creating *The Bruce Poetry Project,* which you can find here:

https://thebruceprojects.com/portfolio-item/the-bruce-poetry-project/

Why do people enjoy my poems?

I admit I am not totally sure, but they tell me that there are a few reasons:

Some are just fun to hear, especially when read aloud.

Some make people think about something in a different way.

However, I think the biggest reason people enjoy—and benefit from—my poems is they are experiencing my life with me.

I don't mean to say that my life is more interesting than anyone else's; however, I do mean to say that I am reaching inside of myself, about what I am thinking, experiencing, and feeling, and telling about this in a poetic format.

I think people benefit from seeing into the soul of another person, and my poems give readers that gift. This is really me, completely unfiltered, the way only poetry can be.

And what is special about me is that I continuously find things that are impossible to do, and then I try really hard to do them anyway. Sometimes I am successful and sometimes I fail. I admit that I like success a lot better than failure, but both are okay. The Flying Pig title is a metaphor for all these attempts.

What is also special about me is my hobby, which has been since my mid-teens, to just think about *stuff*, with the goal being to come up with thoughts that haven't been thought before. And the Flying Pig is a metaphor for that too.

Finally, I will say this about poetry: It is a transformational art form. It is taking a deep thought about almost anything the poet finds important or interesting or inspiring and painting the thought into something truly beautiful, meaningful, and inspirational, all the while using words as the paintbrush. Before leaving this introduction, I will let you know that letting out my inner performing artist, I have posted a reading of these poems on **YouTube**. All you have to do is go on **YouTube**, click

The Bruce Poetry Project, and you can see me performing. I do warn you: Leonardo DiCaprio I am certainly not, but you might have fun watching me trying my best and flubbing just a bit.

Okay, now let's read some poems . . .

THE HAT—SOMEONE REALLY SHOULD TELL HIM

He bought a hat—a hat he bought
It gave him just the look he sought

Out he came from haberdashing
Thinking that he looked so smashing

Down the street he walked on air
Filled he was with savoir faire

Then on home to his sweet wife
She saw him proud and full of life

“Oh lord my God!” she almost blurted
Quick she turned with face averted

Now what to do and how to handle
The man she loved but not put out his candle?

He prized her honesty—she’d give him no lies
But if she were honest, she’d see puppy dog eyes

The choice so tough it was Hobson-worthy
What should she do about this awful derby?

To wait a day was the easy decision
He'd be off to work and there meet derision

The chapeau'd be gone and off his head
And she'd not be blamed for a word she'd said

The morning next dawned after the night
Off to work he went and he looked so bright

In he strutted, gentleman through and through
And the topper he wore was snappy and new

No surprise was his office mates' conclusion
There'd be no upside to speak ill of his head's protrusion

No doubt he'd get an earful from his missus
She'd set him straight or he'd get no kisses

No need at work their colleague to ruffle
For plain speaking could cause a kerfuffle

Now imbued with pride through tacit endorsement
His headpiece had received only positive reinforcement

This confirmed his view that the hat was a winner
He'd take it out that night for a formal dinner

His wife said with only slight hint of persuasion
"Maybe a Fedora was more appropriate for the occasion?"

In response he beamed—he couldn't wait to doff
His new wardrobe addition—'twas a chance to show it off

So out they went, a well-dressed pair
Except for the piece that covered his hair

'Twas no surprise their closest friends that night
Said not a single word about the sight

Whether sombrero, Stetson, stove pipe, ten-gallon, or lid
'Twasn't their place to remark, to make fun, or kid

And when all his friends, kin, and colleagues were done
None said a bad word, none would spoil his fun

As time passed by it was more of a waste
To imply his hat choice wasn't fine of taste

And so it went on over many long years
He wore it with pride, without the slightest of fears

Finally, one and all accepted that
The hat was him and he was the hat

After all, maybe it didn't look that bad
And it made the man they all loved happy and glad

What can I say—I love hats. I have a whole bunch of them and I keep buying them. Sometimes people say, I love that hat, but I wonder if they secretly are chuckling behind my back.

Also, I do love this poem. I think it might be my all-time favorite. It is partly its dorky and awkward and happy message, but it is also the bouncy rhythm. For some reason I just love reading it again and again—especially aloud. If you read it aloud to a friend, I urge you to read it at a good pace. Oh, and wear a hat when you read it!

I MAY BE AN ASSHOLE, BUT . . .

Sometimes when you want to reach your goal
What you need the most is a total asshole

When you feel like quitting and just want to sob
You can call your asshole to do the job

Instead of sympathizing with all your whining
I'll kick your butt and stop your pining

When you need a hug for your bonhomie
Go on home and tell your mommy

Cause I'm not here to kiss your ass
I'm around to give you gas

For the best thing you need to keep your clock ticking
Is a good old-fashioned hard ass-kicking

I know you won't like it and I'll be on my own
Since no one likes getting shoved from a comfort zone

I'm sure there are others who'll extoll your wonder
My only plan is to make you thunder

Will you thank me someday? To be fair
I love you enough that I simply don't care

So I may be an annoying boor in playing this role
But I'm on your side—I'm your asshole

The heart of this poem is to say that by my being an asshole to you, I am showing you a deeper love and caring than even your parents would give you. This is because I am risking my relationship with you by being too honest and taking the risk that I will lose you in the end.

I find myself in this role a fair amount, and being honest, I don't like it at all. It is often shoving someone out of a comfort zone, which means causing the other person discomfort. Even if I feel in my heart I am benefiting the other person, the other person usually resents me either openly or subtly, so I do feel like an asshole, and I just don't like that feeling—not one bit.

This is the ultimate gift that one human can give to another, isn't it? But it sucks to give the gift.

I'M A BAD BOY—AREN'T I?

Beneath the smile that's on my face
I long to be in another place

Where I could strike the mother lode
Do as I wish with my own moral code

Instead of following rules that render me toothless
I could do anything at all, including being ruthless

I'd treat the laws like a relic and a token
And care not a whit when by me they were broken

If you got in my way, I'd put you down
You're in my place and this is my town

I'd have sinews of iron and a will of steel
And to the ladies I would greatly appeal

My bad boy persona would be the envy of all
Young and old would be in my thrall

I also mention that this super ego of me
Is on the side of the downtrodden, and I hear their plea

The danger wouldn't be enough for me to play my part
I would also need to have a good heart

Ah, all of this would be amazing—
I look up smiling and stargazing

But then I sigh, as this is all just a thought
As each day I do just what I ought

As I think on it a mistress would cause a lot of trouble
And she would turn my excellent marriage into rubble

And the thought of being chased by those in power
Would keep me up at night and my confidence devour

Not to mention—maybe I'm not that tough
Especially if things got really rough

So in the end my only guilty pleasure
Is to root for TV bad guys at my leisure

This poem was inspired by a TV Show called Peaky Blinders. *The main protagonist is Tommy Shelby, played by Cillian Murphy. He is an utterly ruthless gangster who, at the same time, has a moral compass. This fellow inspires me, as in one sense of ego I want to be him because, well, he is so doggone cool! But at the same time I know I couldn't be him since I don't have the courage to live with that level of uncertainty and stress, which is why, my whole life, I have been essentially a goody-two-shoes.*

MOON POEM

The strawberry moon across the water
Made me pleased to have a daughter

Side by side we stared with wide eyes
At the ethereal presence that fills the skies

What would this sight have meant without
This one I love beyond all doubt?

Inspiring beauty is of little worth
If you're one and alone upon this Earth

'Tis the thrill of meaningful sharing
Of that you see with one you're caring

Otherwise, oh strawberry moon,
My thrill in the moment would turn to gloom

Snug she stands in my shoulder's love
My daughter and me and the moon above

I have a daughter I love so much. She is truly awesome. And one night I was with her by the sea and looking out at the moon shining in deep strawberry color out of a storm that was roiling the ocean where we were watching.

And then I thought of that famous poem, "The Highwayman," with the line: "The moon was a ghostly galleon, tossed upon cloudy seas."

And it inspired me to try—well, not to do better, but to do something that reflected the moon that we were seeing. And then this came to me.

Yes, my daughter loves this poem as much as I do, and sometimes we tear up when we read it.

MY DEMONS COME AT NIGHT

The sun is out and it's time to revel
Nothing to fear—no thoughts of the devil

But now today's ending—the sun's coming down
My uplifted smile turns into a frown

There's naught going wrong—all things seem just fine
But now look at the clock—it's near half past nine

Soon it will be night, and my carefree will vanish
Darkness will take me—bad thoughts I can't banish

My head will hit pillow and I'll be off to sleep
As I fall in the abyss, evil things creep

When the realm of dreams is in control
I can't use iron will to protect heart nor soul

Why oh why when darkness doth call
All around me wrong things befall?

Inside the depths of my imagination
Some truly awful physical devastation

Or a simple concern that I'll be embarrassed
By screwing up big time—my ego will be harassed

Fear of failure, of death, or being left all alone
Or—worst of all—fear of the unknown

Now something is chasing me
And strongly outpacing me

It's coming nearer and closer—I can feel its breath
Too close now, and it feels like death

The night has left me all shuddering wet
As I finally wake up all soaked in cold sweat

Gasping a bit, up to weavy feet I can lumber
What was it then that disturbed all my slumber?

Perhaps I am lucky that I cannot recall
Just what it was that caused such a squall

A smile bursts now upon my face
Nothing more doth me chase

The morning is here and it's brightest day
The night is now many hours away

A friend of mine and I were speaking one day about how terrifying dreams can be, that even if your life is going just fine, you cannot control your dreams. Happily, I rarely have scary dreams, but, once in a while, we all do. This is about that.

TEEN POEM

We're just plain parents, you know what I mean
We have us a daughter, who's now a teen

Things are great, at least so far
But the boy that she's dating, he's not a star

Unwashed and slimy with oily hair
And his stoned expression leaves naught to care

Unworthy so clear of our precious daughter
Whose sweetness and beauty are pure as glacier water

As her dad I thought it made sense to point out
The boy's many faults, so she'd share my doubt

"Not the best plan," said my much wiser wife
She had more insight to avoid teenage strife

"Speak not a word about it," she admonished me
"There'll be the right moment, and then you will see

"Otherwise, if you push forward your point
Deeper wonder with the boy you'll anoint"

"OK," I agreed with reluctance, as I knew she was smarter
And I put a pin in my usual Triple-A self-starter

It was only a week or so later we were abed in state
The boy phoned to inform us that our girl would be late

"What's the reason, pray tell?" asked my wife in feigned
lighthearted mood
"Ah," said the boy, oh too quickly, "she's a bit ill from
eating Indian food"

"OK, of course," said my wife as she hung up the phone
"This is it"—she smiled as if she'd already known

I looked her askance with my thoughts all a muddle
She calmed me down and said, "Don't get in a befuddle

"Just wait a bit more and let's see it play out"
"OK," I said, though my face made clear my doubt

Sure as shooting, the phone rang once more
"Perhaps," said the boy, it was best if we came to his door

"Nothing to worry," he added nonchalant
But best if we took her home from his haunt

So now out of bed and into the car
Not a long drive, since he didn't live far

When we got there, things looked a lot worse
She'd puked on his rug and he was trying not to curse

We bundled our girl into the back seat
Hugged and crying and bedraggled, the poor thing was beat

As I put it in drive, the boy asked, "What of my rug?"
    in parental fear
The answer needed little thought since it was crystal
    line clear

"Since it was you that got our girl in this way,
Seems like it's your problem"—and we drove away

We got her home quick and put her to bed on the double
But of course we asked what had caused all the trouble

The Indian food story was scarce to be believed
"Pray tell us so we can be relieved"

"Mom and Dad, a cigar was all that we did smoke
Not of anything wrongful did I take a toke"

"What was in the cigar?" I watched her eyes so innocent
    wide
"It was just tobacco" our now-recovering girl neatly replied

"Oh, bullshit!" my wife and I said together—"Now tell us
    the truth—
It was filled up with marijuana, now sayeth sooth"

At long last, with tears, she did confess
'Twas a "blunt" she had smoked which made all the mess

I admit at this point it was hard for us to look worried
With plastered-on frowns back to our bedroom the two
of us hurried

We stifled our laughter and our broad smiles
And I doffed an imaginary hat at her strategic beguiles

The boy we thought so much of was never again seen
Rain dance—rain dance—he was gone from our teen

Better yet, the next morning we lied to our girl
We said pot smoking often causes this kind of a swirl

And it took the better part of a year for her to figure out
It was the tobacco—not the pot—that caused her redoubt

So happy we were this one time to outwit our teen
A parental triumph—and you know what I mean

This poem tells a story and I give my word it is really true and accurate.

If you have teenagers—if you have friends with teenagers—or if you can remember when you were a teenager—or if you are currently a teenager (is that everyone?)—then this poem should resonate with you.

I will say that no one hears it without chuckling or laughing out loud.

THE BLANK PAGE

What frightens a writer more than anything—a blank page

What inspires a writer more than anything—a blank page

What is a blank page anyway? It's the beginning of everything, isn't it?

The ultimate challenge in life is turning that blank page into something worthwhile

Your very life itself begins as a blank page and you get to write the story

Ahhhh—a blank page just like this one was just a few minutes ago, but now . . .

To be consistent with the concept of this poem, I will not make a note about it.

THE BUTT-DIAL

He'd been fifty years old for now quite a while
And it was a pretty good life, he thought with a smile

But one small big thing did his contentment defile
His daughter—now full grown—had left his domicile

His memories floated back to when she was a child
He recalled very well she was complex and versatile

Deeper reflection only sharpened the trial
Alone now he felt, like on a desert isle

But just as his thoughts had come closer to vile
He jumped up in joy, no longer hostile

'Twas the phone now abuzz and his heart raced a mile
His daughter was calling her dad—what a smile!

"Hello! Hello! Hello!" he answered with questions compiled
Then—oh no—he saw it was just a butt-dial

Pause . . .

At first he sighed deeply, with thoughts filled with bile
But then—what the heck—he just pressed redial

If you are a parent and your kid has grown up and left the nest, odds are you will find yourself in this situation. You may have thought you have pride and self-esteem, but somehow you end up in the place I find myself in with this poem. Oh well.

FUCK IT!

I knew I'd have no chance
If I asked that girl to dance

And I knew without a doubt
I'd never win the boxing bout

No chance I'd be elected
I might as well have just defected

And what a silly notion
If I tried for that promotion

But before I kick the bucket
Why not try and just say fuck it?

This poem is a lot more important than its throw-away title makes it seem.

It came to me from a book I read long ago called The Heart of a Fighter. *In the book, the protagonist was trying to decide whether to take a fight in MMA when he knew the other guy was just better. He went back and forth with his decision, but then these two words—"fuck it"—made the decision for him. He won the fight, by the way, because the other guy was unprepared. Go figure that.*

For me this is a metaphor for the way I want to live the rest of my life. After all, the biggest regrets are the chances you never took. Remember from above that the one regret the World's Most Interesting Man wants to have is to not know the feeling of regret, so . . . fuck it!!!

GREAT

Am I out of juice or just getting started?
Are there clouds ahead or does the sun keep them parted?

Here I am in my seventh decade
I don't need to work—I've got it made.

What's the meaning now for what I do?
My friends are retired and I should be too

But isn't the point of dyin' and livin'
Accomplishing something and being driven?

I'm torn—indecision on what really matters
Working at my age would be mad as hatters

Maybe—just maybe—I've done enough
I've pushed so hard and I've made it rough.

But stopping is dying will be my fate
That it sucks is what makes it great

I love this poem as it is inspiring to me. I crafted a saying: "It Sucks is What Makes it Great."

On the one hand, the saying makes no grammatical sense, as you can easily see, but on the other hand it makes perfect sense the more you think about it.

Tom Hanks (sort of) said it in the movie A League of Their Own, when he was talking to Geena Davis about baseball. His exact words were, "The hard is what makes it great."

My saying is close to that and evolves from that movie plus a note from a book called Living with a Seal, where the Seal (David Goggins) says, "If it doesn't suck, we don't do it."

In any case, the point is that without some pain to "earn" whatever you are trying to accomplish, it is hardly "great," is it? The greatness is—somehow—inextricably tied into the difficulty (suckiness) you endured to get there.

All of this inspires me to try to do great things and not to be too shattered when a good percentage of the time I fail. The greatness of the successes more than makes up for the failures.

WHY IS A FRIEND?

I'm a quick study
When I think of my buddy

He'll be there for me
If I'm up a tree

I'll cry on his shoulder
If I'm hit by a boulder

He'll pick me up when I'm down
He's always around

And he'll make me feel lucky
When my life seems so sucky

Why does he do this for someone like me?
Do I deserve it? What can it be?

I thought hard about it but couldn't tell why
I guess I should ask him and give that a try

So, my dear buddy, answer me straight
Why are you my friend, my wingman, my mate?

He sighed when I asked, as he hadn't a clue
Best he could say was, "What else would I do?"

As a separate endeavor, I have been writing a book on the subject of friendship. It will be published at some point with the title How to Do Friendship.

As I delved into the meaning of friendship, I realized that friends are the most important thing in my life. This is an excerpt from that book, which is poetic enough that I think it is okay to include it here:

> I wonder if just maybe friendship and friends are an explanation of that elusive concept of the meaning of life. At one point or another we all stand on our terrace or our deck or in our backyard or on the roof of our apartment building or in a field somewhere and look up at the sky and ask God, or whoever else we might look to, these questions:
>
> What's life all about? What's going on here? What matters? What is really important? What is the meaning of life?
>
> And we come away from these communing moments sometimes feeling full and satiated and happy, and sometimes empty and aching. But maybe if, when we look up into the night sky, we think about our friends and our friendships, we might feel pretty doggone good about all of it. This is what has been happening to me.

As my book concludes, there may not be a perfect answer to what a friend really is, but this poem has tendrils that say quite a bit about it.

FALSE DREAMS

My brain gets oh so fuzzy
With a drink—then I get buzzy

I find myself so smitten
With the amazing words I've written

I dare not self-admonish
Instead my words I find astonish

'Til I wake up on the next day
And then it seems passé

I wonder as I write this
Is this just more detritus?

I'll know it when I wake
Oh, for goodness' sake!

Well the background here is obvious—I was sitting in a bar writing poems, which is something I do a lot. And as I wrote—and got more inebriated—I started to wonder how this poem would look

in the morning. As I surveyed it in the morning's light, I was doubtful whether it was deep enough to compete with Keats or Nash or Poe for greatness.

INDIFFERENCE

I am but a splintered boat broken on the rocky shoreline of her indifference

Even after the wooden wreckage strews about me, bobbing up and down, I still look to shore in forlorn hope of rescue

But it is not to come, as slowly I sink beneath the waves—for my last look our eyes meet

Was there perhaps a flicker of interest there at my passing?

I am fated not to know

I don't know what inspired this. Well, I guess I do know, but it is not something I want to talk about. It is depressing, isn't it? I was debating whether to include it in this book, but as I was about to exclude it, I realized that it just makes you think, even if the thoughts aren't good ones.

IT WAS SO VERY LONG AGO

Once, as counselor, I took my client's side
The matter was important so I could not let it slide
But the other party was much offended
Perhaps he thought his honor was contended
Words were exchanged and the battle escalated
With the result being a man who me hated
What it was caused the kerfuffle
I remember not—just that it was a scuffle
I guess we went at it toe to toe
It was so very long ago

The end result of the shouting match
Was that long-term enmity did from it hatch
Each of us knew 'twould be a grave mistake
For our paths to cross—trouble 'twould make
People would ask me through the years
Over perhaps a couple of beers
"Why the angry face and eye-rolling look?
What was it caused the donnybrook?"
"Tsk tsk," I'd shrug as if to show
It was so very long ago

Fast forward to the present day
A friend conveyed to my dismay
Another insult from my long ago foe
He'd remarked I was a "so and so"
To my friend it was quite a surprise
I could see it there within his eyes
Had I now fallen in his estimation
To perhaps a somewhat lower station?
Maybe there was a reason my foe thought me so low
Although it was so very long ago

My emotions and my anger quickened
And my hot blood boiled and quickly thickened
I was not someone with whom to trifle
In days of yore I would have grabbed my rifle
I knew I had to strike him hard
Perhaps I would call him a tub of lard
Sublime would be my jubilation
If I could but cause him humiliation
But it's hard to find worthy insult for someone you hardly know
And as I've already mentioned, it was so very long ago

What was it then that stayed my hand?
This attack upon me could and should not stand
Was it rational thought knowing nothing good
Would come from further conflict in my neighborhood?
Was I just tired of keeping up feud
When it just upset my quietude?
Or was I just getting too soft
To keep the game ball longer aloft?
He was likely no more a tub of lard than was I a "so and so"
And after all, it was so very long ago

So with trembling hand, I typed sinner to sinner
"How about you and I go out to dinner?
The many years we've been on opposing teams
We've missed out on what good can come from cooperating, it seems
With your dealmaking skills I can find no flaw
And I am no slouch when it comes to the law
Telling you the truth I cannot recall
What in the deeps of time caused our squall
Do you still remember? I do not know—
And it was so very long ago"

So I went out with my proffer of detente
With a moral imperative worthy of Kant
I stewed and simmered, thinking of dinner
Would my suggested path turn out a winner?
Or perhaps the many insults through our careers
Would result in just some answering jeers
Possibly instead of food and comity sated
I would just be further humiliated
I hardly knew the man or his status quo
And as I've mentioned several times now, it was so very long ago

Upon my countenance there came a great smile
When I received his reply in a very short while
For he said he had "the greatest respect"
Not least for my taking the first step to deflect
Further negativity between us—it was time to detox
"After all, we are playing in the same sandbox
Let us dine instead and toast the future
And our mutual wounds we will happily suture"
He said, "Let's shake hands and unstring the crossbow
It was so very long ago"

So out we went upon the town
Smiles and laughter and nary a frown
Apologies were not even needed
Since to mutual relief hostility had receded
Instead we spoke of how we might help each other
Being now good friends, and with the scotch talking,
    maybe a brother
We toasted, joked, and laughed till dinner ended
And after the evening I was befriended
Sometimes good from bad can flow
And, after all, it was so very long ago

This was the second poem I wrote. I recall writing it about ten years ago. I was in a bar—yes, it seems like I am in bars a lot—but I don't actually drink that much. I guess I just like the bar scene for some reason. I think it allows me to be part of—and observe—humanity as it really is.

But within the framework of this book being my life poem, what is interesting here is that this story actually happened, and the poem details with solid accuracy a story of the triumph of classiness over idiocy, and I am proud of how I acted. Sadly, my counterpart passed away a couple of years ago.

I hope you enjoyed the story.

IT'S YOUR JOB

There are more and more days that I hate my work
I go through the motions and feel like a jerk

Why, oh why, do I do what I do?
I'm really good at it and that is true

But it's just no fun is my despair
My life sucks and it's just not fair

Oh now, slap my face, you little whiner
You've got a job to do, what could be finer?

You're doing that for which you're born
Cut the 'tude that you're so forlorn

You're not being paid to like your work
Too much inward focus, it makes you a jerk

Perhaps a twist of the dial will change your view
And the meaning of work, will in you renew

This is one of those kicks in the ass we all need sometimes. I read this when I am in a whiny mood about work. As someone told me once in a book I read, "You're not paid to like your job—you're paid to do your job."

Somehow, when I think of that, my sense of purpose returns and I am energized again.

LAST CALL

I'm at the bar with so many friends
It'll be a great night that never ends

We drink and drink and drink some more
One of my buddies is stretched out on the floor

One by one they peel away
And I see that I'm the one to stay

My first thought is I that should go home
And not sit here by myself so alone

But now it's the sweetest time of all
I'm with my truly best friend 'til last call

Yikes, another poem from the bar. You will definitely think I have a drinking problem. Should I admit I am having a glass of wine while I type this very sentence?

It's a nice poem, nonetheless—espousing the joy I (sometimes) have in my own company.

LONELY GUY IN A SUIT AND A TIE

"Why, oh why?" I say with a sigh
"Am I the only one left in a suit and a tie?"

Should it be that I claim that the reason
Is 'cause suits and ties are always in season?

Or am I just a man who likes to stand out?
I am awfully stubborn, without any doubt

Possibly I'm like an old car with fins on the fender
And a suit makes it clear what is right for my gender

Could it be that suits are aging protection
As their folds will enhance my mirrored reflection?

Or is it the confidence it brings me as a man about town
Who—without a doubt—would never dress down?

No doubt that when people see me as we pass
They think, There goes a guy with a good bit of class

Worse yet—it may be it makes me think I am better
Than others around me—I'm a stronger go-getter

Or am I just trying to make up for the sins of my youth
When I dressed like a slob and was very uncouth?

Yes—I've figured it out it must be this at last
It's my constant desire to live in the past

Synthesizing my thoughts now all together
I'm in a suit and a tie in all kinds of weather

Now to conclude why try to look so well
So sorry, my reader, I choose not to tell

For some reason I find myself seemingly the last guy in New York City who wears a suit and a tie every day. It is strange, but the sloppier everyone else gets, the more energized I am to take careful stock of my appearance. I spend a lot on clothes and have essentially become something of a clothes-horse.

As a kid I was a slob, so this makes no sense, but so it is.

This poem is my lament.

NO REPLY

Did you ever have that feeling
That sends your senses reeling?
And the more you do reflection
Still your life has no direction?
The most fearful word is "Why?"
As it's the cause of why you try
But if there's no answer to that question
It causes intellectual indigestion
Pause . . .
Maybe this way of thinking
Should be replaced with heavy drinking
Since not every question needs reply
Why not just let this one lie?

This is a scary poem—a very scary poem -- as there is nothing more terrifying than having no purpose. I mean things with no purpose shouldn't really exist, should they?

So this poem bubbled out of that fear, but as I wrote it I had that cold feeling that there wasn't going to be an answer—or a happy ending—to the poem. And instead of deeper reflection, maybe running away from the thinking made more sense.

POEM FOR A REAL MAN

It's pitch black outside, but I hear the surf on the shore
It's quite a cold January—going out would be poor

In my cozy beach house a fire is roaring
A cliché it is how the weather I'm ignoring

A book in my lap and I've the place all alone
I can do what I wish with no one to pick a bone

I look out the window—it's all black and nothing's calling
Time to think about a late evening snack and ignore the
squalling

How fortunate I am to be such a man
Who has fortified himself with such an excellent plan

My biggest concern long about midnight
Is which whiskey to choose—oh what a plight!

But as I look at the single malts inhabiting my shelf
My bonhomie vanishes along with my sense of self

For what's life about but a series of events
That are challenges all or it makes no sense?

Would a real man just sit inside with a scotch
Or run and jump in the sea wearing nothing but his watch?

What an idiotic thought—as I push it away
But there's no one around, no one to gainsay

Now let's take another look at those fine single malts
And put my mind away from the frigid water full of salts

But it's Poe who wrote about the Imp of the Perverse—
The more you consider the implications, the more it gets worse

I recall that when younger I never feared the odds
I was Superman and could take on the gods

But now as an almost-sixty-year-old man
Should I be more reticent, maybe more of an also-ran?

Or should my machismo triumph over common sense?
There's no one around, which adds to the suspense

"What's wrong with me?" I say as I watch my hands pour
    me a double
Should I sip my favorite whiskey or go out and seek trouble?

No one not crazy would take such a self-appointed dare
But to me that makes it all so much better—not fearing the scare

Alone I'd be in the depths, floating and freezing
When I sprang from the water, I'd be cold and wheezing

A heart attack could then kill me shortly
I looked down at my paunch—alas, just a little portly

But to tell my friends I was so much braver
That I, nearing sixty, didn't flinch nor waver

Would that be worth this crazy chance?
It would indeed, so I set down the scotch and pulled
down my pants

The greatest achievements ever done by man
Aren't thought through too deeply with the most perfect
plan

Now off with my shirt and my underwear
There are clubs for this kind of thing with names like
"Polar Bear"

I grab me a towel as I leave the house
It might be useful after a seawater douse

I run out the door, forcing my brain not to think
The rush of frigid air hits me, but I do not blink

Towards the beach I speed, undeterred
I run all the faster, arms outstretched and free as a bird

The ocean laughs as it sees me coming hard and fast
It's seen this game before—the die has been cast

I drop the towel and blast forward, legs a'churning
I can feel the thrill, with my muscles burning

"Do not think!" I shout to my brain in my euphoric state
It's the one organ saying, "Turn back before it's too late!"

I can't help but scream when I make the splash
Prepared as I thought I was, it's still a hard smash

Submerged I am for a second, but it's long enough
So I can tell everyone that, "Yes, I am tough"

Then I struggle from the water, I fight the undertow
It's back to where I started or a cold death, as I know

A moment of panic—where is the shore?
I can't stand the cold water for one moment more

Then I see the beach just where I had left
Towel in the sand—I wasn't bereft

I'm now shaking to my core but feeling oh, so jolly
Now will God reward or punish me for my folly?

I'm just a puny mortal risking it all
Challenging fate, by heeding the call

I run home fast in my birthday suit
Towel flapping 'round in hot pursuit

The door opens and warm air hits me with a gust of joy
I'm a middle-aged man with the heart of a boy

And there on the shelf where my head is turned
Is my double scotch, which now I have earned

Okay, I'm an idiot, I think as I sip and muse
To my body I've given some demented abuse

But in the end I feel so completely gifted
It was worth every bit—I'm now so uplifted

Yes, this is an absolutely true story and I hope you enjoyed it.

Well, the story is almost true. I kept my bathing suit on and did it during the day rather than at midnight, but otherwise I am faithfully relating the tale.

I was alone in Cape May in January when I wrote the poem, and I was about to press "send" to my wife, but then I thought I would hold off until I actually returned from my sea-water douse and could confirm to her that I was actually still alive. I didn't want to freak her out.

This poem emphasizes that there is a fine line between machismo and utter stupidity, and that fine line is defined in hindsight.

Revealing perhaps too much information about myself, it is also me seeking to be an amazing person on some level. Of course, intellectually it likely proves the reverse, but maybe you get my meaning here anyway.

PRETTY AND PLAIN

Only pretty girls get to sit at the bar
I see this as I sit, from afar

It's just not fair to not be anointed
With enough good looks to be so appointed

For men to chase to be their mate
Oh, how sad a plain girl's fate

In her heart, she may offer much more
But we men don't care—we're such a bore

All we want is a cute babe to cuddle
Really stupid and just a befuddle

If only God could take away the veil
I think plain girls would be the holy grail

I was thinking one day as an unattractive woman walked by about how unfair life was. In her mind and heart she might be wonderful, but we men don't seem to value that, and by making that decision we are missing out.

I was accused of inadvertently being sexist with this poem, when of course I meant the exact opposite. I almost didn't include it for that reason but then thought perhaps the fact that it gave rise to feelings made it a good inclusion after all. You can judge.

PRIDE POEM

As I think on this, let me begin
To say pride in itself is no sin

What is wrongful about pride
Is overstating what you supplied

As pride may falsely convince
That you are really a prince

You've put too much stock in your self worth
When it's really just the luck of your birth

It means little if you were born handsome, strong, or smart
It's what you've done, or not done, that may set you apart

Now that that's out of the way
Let me go on further to say

That if you're not deceived
By what you've achieved

And it's not just birth luck
But done by hard work and pluck

Then it's okay to revel
And not a bit from the Devil

You've a right to have pride
Since you fought for the ride

Now that that is explained
For sexism I can be blamed

By focusing now on man
And his possible life plan

And I say a man may walk tall and proud
If with love of woman he be endowed

Indeed, a woman of depth, strength, and heart
Sets the man who wins her apart

And it's no sin of pride
To tell the world far and wide

For some reason, the concept of pride interests me. I know it is supposed to be a sin, but I think that is incorrect. The sin pertains to wrongfully overstated pride or, a new word I invented: "overpride."

For me at least, feeling good, and even great, about what I have accomplished is perfectly fine and good. I find it harder to explain this in my note on this poem than in the poem itself.

PRIDE POEM NUMBER TWO

Should I be proud to be a beauty
Or should I be proud to do my duty
Even when I didn't want to?

Should I be proud that I am smart
Or that I have a good heart
Even when I didn't need to?

Should I be proud I made a lot of money
Or that I have the love of my honey
Even when I took her for granted?

Should I be proud of my work
Or that I try not to be a jerk
Even when I'm under stress?

In the end, I've resolved to only fully boast
If family and friends stay always close
Even when it's only me

This is another poem about the concept of pride and in my view a deep poem. Well, at least it was deep for me. I was thinking about what people are actually proud of compared with what they truly deserve to be proud of, and there is quite a dichotomy.

As for me, if I find a person I really respect and that person wants to love me (as my wife) or be my friend, I find that the most enthralling thing, and it makes me the proudest.

By the way, I devote a chapter to this concept in my upcoming book: How to Do Friendship.

QUICK POEM—SAYS IT ALL

I saw a little lizard

The little fellow scurried by

I bet his life is much more peaceful

Because he doesn't wonder why

A poem doesn't have to be long to be meaningful, and this one seems to embody that concept pretty well. Yes, I was sitting in a lounge chair at a Florida pool when this occurred and inspired a poem.

REFLECTIONS

He was older now but not yet old
A life of great fortune had favored his bold

Time, he reflected, hadn't taken its toll
He was hale in his strength, both body and soul

But something was nagging, something was bugging
At the corner of mind, something was tugging

He'd hit every pinnacle, smashed every ball
Now it brought him up short—was this all?

No more could be done in his chosen profession
He'd hit the tippy top with ease of accession

What would it gain him—yet another accolade?
The adrenaline buzz had long begun to fade

Never before had he felt so frail
Now too much success just felt like a fail

Too late it is now to start something new
But continuing on causes a feeling of blue

I'm stuck a crossroads, I'm all in a dither
Where should I go now—yonder or hither?

For hour after hour he drank whiskey and beer
Hoping the liquor would assuage his fear

At last it hit him—*I shan't be a loser*
'Tis the scotch that is talking, but I can be a chooser

Perhaps he'd earned time to reflect on success
And lay down the burden before more became less

Yes, that is the answer to my deepest ponder—
I don't need to force myself hither and yonder

Instead I'll just sit right here for a while
Nursing my drink with a beatific smile

Yet another poem about a man drinking scotch—I really need to look into that, don't I? Putting that aside, this poem was me digging into myself. I have had a good—I guess great—career, and I was wondering, "What next?"

Being honest with myself, I couldn't think what would be next, which concerned me a bit, and then I thought maybe it was just fine after all.

ROADSIDE POEM

It was the city of Charleston I was heading towards
And on the highway there were many billboards

There were rest stops, hotels, and advertising, it's true
But many from Jesus, whose love shone through

At first his messages seemed heaven sent
But then one shouted out that I should repent

I took it all with a grain of salt
As being Jewish, it wasn't my fault

But then things changed from looking out for humanity—
I was kind of thinking I'd lost my sanity

The love I'd felt from Jesus had been replaced
By personal injury lawyer signs that the road defaced

There were so many and the contrast was jarring
From love and faith to fighting and warring

The message to teach insurance companies a lesson
Not as uplifting as a godly confession

The whole episode pulled my thoughts asunder
What's it all about? I must admit, I wonder

In early 2025, I took a cross-country trip, trying to emulate Kerouac, and really trying to learn what America was truly about.

This poem—a bit silly but from real life—was one of the things that struck me along the way. It's the opposite of deep, but it certainly is interesting, isn't it?

AMERICA—A NEW YORKER'S THOUGHTS

A would-be Kerouac I went to hit the Midwest
Wondering if there I'd find America's worst or its best

On the coasts some call them fly-over states
Denigrated as not with us—they're not our mates

Ask the *Times, Wash Post* or other news sources
They're not worthy of us on our moral high horses

I always wondered if that made real sense
Or was this just an elitest defense?

There was nothing to do but see for myself
So I drove away from the continental shelf

Just me and a car full of changes of dress
I wanted to fit in, I must confess

I hit Nashville, Memphis, Tulsa, and Austin
The polar opposites of New York, LA, and Boston

I went to these places in the US interiors
Thought by coastals to be full of racists and moral inferiors

But when I saw these places all in the raw
Just friendly warm people was all I saw

Only friendship, and much more, from these faux brigands
beamed
I felt they're my peeps after all, just as I dreamed

But it wasn't that simple, after all, to assess
There's more to tell if you'll hear my confess

It hit me recalling a quick vignette
'Twas while in Austin I had a small tête-à-tête

I made a safety remark for a biker's child
Then the father cursed me out and strongly reviled

I was taken aback—I admit it threw me
So out of place it made me feel gloomy

I related this story to an Austiner that very day
He was vexed and embarrassed I'd been treated that way

"That's not the actions of a self-respecting Texan," he
vehemently said
"The guy's a California transplant, as that's how they're bred"

I digested his indignation with a grain of salt
Quick was the Texan to put a coastal city at fault

I now knew it all in my reflections
That the seeming contempt flows in both directions

The epiphany for me was now made plain
So upsetting it is, and it's just insane

It's the news we're getting, which is truly horrific
Debasing us all to each other instead of calling us terrific

Bad views don't just sit alone on the coasts
And not in the middle, either, despite similar boasts

It's a two-way street for our divisions
We all need some major revisions

And this won't happen if we stay in one place
We'll just get fake news that the good will erase

I urge us all to get 'round and enjoy the nation's pleasures—
Its people, of course, who are wonderful treasures

All around me as I drove through the land
Those I met were just so grand

Those whom I met were only the best
From all directions—south, north, east and west

In 2024 I started to think about politics. Well, I mean I had always thought about politics, just like everyone does, with my chief contribution being annoying my friends with bitching (or even ranting) about whatever was being done wrong by those in charge of the state or the country or the world. Why couldn't everyone just be as smart as me?

But really all I was doing was whining behind the scenes. And then someone gave me a quote from Plato: "Participate in government or be governed by those who do." And I had an epiphany—that whining in the back rooms was not going to work for me. So I resolved to get involved.

It took a bit, but after some real soul-searching I realized that I didn't know everything after all, and sitting in the ultimate elitist paradise of New York City was not going to make me an effective leader, so I decided to go on Walk-About (from the Crocodile Dundee *movie). Since I did my Walk-About in a car, it was more of a Drive-About across as much of the country as I could cover—I think I hit about 15 states.*

This poem came about from my trip—and yes, it is the same trip as in the preceding "Roadside Poem."

RUB-A-DUB-DUB

Rub-a-dub-dub
I'm sitting in a pub

Doing some thinking
And some drinking

It's early in the day
But, after all, what the hey?

This day doesn't matter
If I'm thin or getting fatter

I think I'll buy another round
But there is no friend around

I could buy one for a stranger
But that kind of feels like danger

So I'll just drink alone
Quiet as a stone

Rub-a-dub-dub
I'm sitting in a pub

Does every poem have to have depth and meaning? If so, then you could skip this one. This is just me—yes in a pub—enjoying my own company and being perfectly happy about it.

THE LAST CHANCE

Off to work in the early morn
Gone I am before the dawn

Then at night I'm home after dark
My job's a challenge, not a walk in the park

A wife and two daughters are the stated reason
That I work so hard, no matter the season

No time for me with them to have any fun
Sorry, my girls, duty calls and I've gotta run

"Why, Mommy, do we never get to see our dad?
Doesn't he like us, or is he mad?"

"No, my honeys," Mom replies dutifully
"He loves us all dearly, oh so beautifully."

But in her eyes they can see the lie
The lonely stream is passing by

Her man, he works from sun to sun
Always work and no time for fun

Pre-school, middle school, high school pass in a blur
The girls I loved so much aren't what they were

My wife has come to be respected in the community
She has many friends and can be without me with impunity

And I'm pleased that my little girls are so much grown
They have so many friends that they're never alone

Sometimes I'm feeling adrift but I'm so content
I know the bond among my girls is strong as cement

They haven't much of a dad but they have each other
So I don't have to worry and don't have to bother

They no longer ask me to recitals and other events
Dad's always too busy, so to do so makes no sense

I wonder am I getting too boring
And too much my family ignoring?

And then at last I'm out of steam
I'm tired now, if you know what I mean

There's no more bullets left in the gun
I've had enough, no more wanting to run

It's time at last to power down
And now be a man about the town

Gladness fills my heart at what I'll pursue
With my girls and me—oh, what we will do!

I'm rushing home on wings of fire
At last, my girls, it's time to retire

Let's go away to sit in the sun
My career is over—now it's time for fun

With flowers in hand and a thrill in my heart—
It's far too long we've been apart

As the door opens up, I feel the first tinge of worry
It seems that the three are going out in a hurry

They're on their way, my girls and my wife
They've much to do and I'm not part of their life

One by one they kiss me as out they run
Long ago—without me—they learned to have their fun

Now I stand beside the empty door
And I see to them I've been a bore

In a flash I turn and run them after
Hearing them full of smiles and laughter

"Please take me along!" I beg them, "Please!"
Though I'm upright, I fall on my knees

Between the three they pass a glance—
Will they give me one last chance?

My breath has stopped while I await
Their decision and my fate

"You know," says wife, "we've waited quite long
But you're a lucky man that our love is strong

"You can come along tonight
The four of us will be a sight"

Heart aflutter, I take a deep breath
Career blindness almost caused my death

What a fool I've been, I now realize
Now fate has cut me down to size

What was I thinking all those years
I missed out on hugging my dears?

As we walk to the car to go to the dance
My wife whispers to me, "It was your last chance"

As noted above, this—almost—happened to me—but didn't!

For that reason, and revealing too much perhaps, I tear up when I read this one.

THE FINAL GOAL LINE

I like to think I am really clever
But my life won't last forever.

So each day I have to live
Is one day less I have to give

Unless I think there's an afterlife
I should care less and less about daily strife

The days ahead are fewer than the past
But there's no reason for me to be downcast

Thus I should say and do what I want
There's no moral imperative—sorry, Immanuel Kant

Just maximize fun, with joy transcend
In the days that remain until the end

I think I'll end up feeling just fine
As I approach the final goal line

I wonder if I am too obsessed with, well, death, as it seems like there are a fair number of poems about the end of my career, my life, etc.

This one is a bit humdrum on the subject.

THE PHILOSOPHER BLUES

I tussled with a moral theory
For hours and hours 'til my brain was weary

Was I right or was I wrong?
Thinking—thinking—takes so long

But 'tis the lot of those who philosophize
To look ambiguity in the face and not deal in lies

I knew an answer just had to be there somewhere
But, pulling out my hair, I can't see it anywhere

Worse still, when I'm sure of conclusion
I realize—alas—that it's just an illusion

At last I give it up—I'm mad at Socrates
Whose singular truth has brought me to my knees

"I'm the wisest man in Athens," said the wily old devil
"Since I know just one thing that is truth on the level

"And that is I that I know for sure that I know nothing at all"
So in a fit of pique, I threw my books against the wall

All my life I wanted to be a philosopher. I love to just sit by the pool with a pad and a pen—and no iPhone—and just think about stuff. But things don't always work out well.

And there is nothing more frustrating than spending an hour—or many hours—or even a week—wrestling with a moral or philosophical theory, totally sure you have something ground-breaking and interesting to say, and then realizing you simply don't. You just painted yourself into an intellectual corner or ran into a brick wall that stops you cold.

And throwing my books against the wall is as good a way of dealing with this situation as any I could suggest.

THE POEM OF BRUCE

There was an old man did a lot
Taking on too much was his spot
'Twas all too much fun
'Til he said, "I am done –
Maybe just one more thing—why not?"

*Well, yes, this is me to a tee. I think I do—or try to do—more things than anyone I have ever heard of. If you don't believe me, go to my Bruce Projects website—*www.thebruceprojects.com*—and see for yourself.*

Am I taking on too much?

Absolutely.

THE VESSEL

Part I—The Dream

He was a young man and he knew it all
In the prime of his life and he heard the call

At that ripe old age—near about twenty
He hadn't enough, and he wanted plenty

It was high time to make to make a critical acquisition—
Someone to enhance his prominent position

He'd work harder than ever a great career to achieve
She'd be by his side and in him would believe

As his world would expand in every which way
She'd be with him every step of his play

Now what were the necessary characteristics?
A bit like a puzzle with relevant logistics

She'd have to be pretty, of course
With a wife who was plain he'd hardly be a force

Intelligent enough and with a calm disposition
Just the right choice for a man in his position

Home she would stay and raise his offspring
A voice that was soothing to the children would sing

She'd love him so well and he would support her
"Now where can she be so I'll be sure to court her?"

Into his sphere a woman to nestle
He needed a wife who would be his vessel

Part II—The Satisfaction

He was in his prime now, not far from fifty
And his life had gone perfect—indeed, pretty nifty

All that he wanted had then been achieved
All from his own efforts, he fully believed

He had money and fame and friends and power
Above all the others he was pleased to tower

A scotch in hand in his easy chair
He was so full of himself he was walking on air

There was little left now with which to wrestle
Happy she'd made him—she was his vessel

Part III—The Wonderment

An older man now in his later years
Career long since over, no time for tears

Old and tired he was, it was time for reflection
"Let's think it through with careful detection"

She'd done a good job, he had to admit
Hardly ever was she one to sit

She'd kissed his cheek when he'd worked late
And happily with a girlfriend she'd make a date

While he slogged and he struggled through long client dinners
She'd loved raising their kids to be happy and winners

While he was late to bed and early to rise
She'd toned herself up with healthy exercise

While he was aged now before his time
His wife, his vessel, was just plain old fine

The years now hung heavy upon his frame
Was it all worth it to achieve money and fame?

The money he'd earned was now set aside
When he was gone for his wife it would well betide

And the friends that gathered 'round them all so often
Would be hers, no doubt, when he was laid in his coffin

She'd been the one to invest so wise
So she'd be just fine after his demise

Part IV—The Realization
Then finally it hit him with a shocking conclusion
Perhaps that his view was just an illusion

He looked at his wife, realizing at last
It was now much too late to relive the past

A coldness came on him as turmoil haunted
It was she and not he who'd created the life she wanted

He'd be leaving much sooner than he had expected
And she'd live much longer, he now reflected

Right from the start, he was right about a vessel
He was hers all along, and nothing so special

This is a pretty creepy poem. I actually scared myself as I wrote it.

From a masculine and even sexist point of view, it takes the position that we men are an awful lot dumber than we think we are. Vive La Dame!

When I discuss it with others, I find that different people have different views of the woman—the wife—in the poem, i.e., did she really get what she wanted?

THE WHY OF WORK

Off to work, so very early, in that special time and space that so few partake of and fewer still can thrill to—why is that?

And then at night, so late it has gotten, but I am still enraptured with more special time, in lieu of home to warmth of wife—why is that?

I am enjoying a potion so subtle that it is an acquired taste, but once acquired there is truly nothing like it. Like a very fine snifter of high octane liquor that it takes a true intrepid to have the temerity to taste, much less savor. I am blessed and my thrills are shown in the jig of my walk and the embrace of my smile

But looming is that pitiless three-letter word that quails my rapture and makes my enjoyment unsavory

Why? As I look through the darkened window . . . dark as night at both ends of the day . . . I ask

I long since have had more than "enough"

Am I at heart grasping, greedy, ungracious, rapacious, base of spirit, and a soul unworthy of respect even from myself?

Or am I glorified personage who has crafted works that feed, inspire, serve, love, and nurture many?

After but a moment of self-doubt, my courage returns and to the pitiless Why? I reply with strength: "Neither villain nor hero am I today, nor will I be tomorrow, nor was I yesterday"

I just treasure the thrill of the hunt . . .

And is that just fine as long as I don't trample the grass too much with the hoofs of my horse?

I wrote this long ago—possibly my first poem, even before I started writing poetry for real—as a younger man sort of in the prime of building a career for myself.

It outlines what I was going through at the time as I was trying hard to convince myself that what I was doing made sense as a life purpose.

TO THE DREAMERS

I laughed when I cried
Melancholy inside

My dream project had failed
And the hurt I bewailed

Failure had me in tatters
I'd neglected other matters

All that I'd sought
Was now just for naught

What is life all about?
I now have much doubt

It's not giving your all
As you've too far to fall

I'd heeded not the naysayers
Those timid non-players

Whose dire maledictions
And negative predictions

Were now proved just right
Oh I'm feeling affright

How, now, can I face them
When last I'd disgraced them

For not being on my team
When I'd promulgated my dream?

I wanted to show them their gaffe
But now they'd have the last laugh

Now I open the door
To those I abhor

To my surprise they are smiling
And acting most beguiling

They want me to join in their revel
Now that I'm down to their level

Never, never! I won't be their whore
Nay, I'll find a new dream and wallow no more

And the next time they'll see
What failure's made of me

I'll not give it a rest
Till I ace the test

I'm stronger than ever
And I'll go on forever

This one is almost too revealing of who I am. This is me naked before you.

TRIUMPH POEM

My life began at sixty-five
At last I knew, at last I was alive

By now it's clear the die is cast
I can see the future and the past is past

So eager I am now for each day
I've no need to strive to make my way

At some point in life you've done what you've done
And now what's left is to have some fun

No need for me to watch each word
I can be a fool, a genius, or a nerd

My tread is firm and my giddiness swells
No more must I need to walk on eggshells?

Time to shine and enjoy the revel
You don't like my 'tude, you can go to the Devil

So at this point I say with glee
What could they possibly do to me?

This is the amazing freedom you get when you hit the top of whatever heap you are trying to climb.

It was inspired by Milton Gould, who is someone you probably haven't heard of. He was one of the most famous litigators in New York City—legendary. In the depths of time—almost forty-five years ago, as a very junior lawyer—I accompanied him to court for a trial. My role was basically to carry his litigation bag.

In the cab down to the courthouse I asked him if he was nervous.

He scoffed at me—a true scoffing—and said imperiously, "What could they ever do to me?"

It was almost forty years later that that vignette inspired this poem.

VERMONT MAGIC

I'm up in Vermont
I can do what I want

But I don't like hiking
And I'm scared of biking

It's okay outdoors
Unless it rains or it pours

I could view the green hills
But just minutes it fills

It's too cold now to swim in the lake
And I don't like to cook or to bake

'Round and 'round the floor I pace
My mind is spinning all over the place

Indeed, I am starting to feel a bit manic
It's worse than that—it's actual panic

I must get back to civilization
There I know my proper station

Vermont is just the biggest bore
The worst of the worst—a complete snore

Then it hits me between the eyes
I'm weak at the knees, ankles, and thighs

I'm so into myself, I end up tragic
For I've totally missed my life's magic

I've no more relevance in New York City
Than out in the country where it's so pretty

If I can find no meaning in contemplation
Then my life itself is a cruel imitation

Now I take another look at what's around
With fervent steps I leap and bound

Baking, hiking, biking in the green hills
It is all just fine—my cup it fills

I feast upon my many alternatives
To each I now have a strong affirmative

I'm up in Vermont
I can do what I want

My wife and I have some very close friends who, unfortunately for us, moved up to Vermont. Although I love them as deepest friends, at first I was concerned about visiting them, as what on earth does anyone do in Vermont, anyway?

My friend told me quite pithily, "This is Vermont—you can do what you want."

And now I can't wait to visit Vermont, see my friends, and truly do what I want.

'TWAS A FAMILY SECRET

'Twas a family secret, it was true
And that meant no one knew

So she only told her mother
And she swore to tell no other

Of course she also told her sister
And her husband when he kissed her

This was by no means spilling the beans
After all, these were not just gossiping teens

They were family members of discretion and high station
Who cared much about their reputation

For holding very confidential
Matters that were consequential

So the matter stayed well hidden
Till the words popped out unbidden

When her mother told her best friends—
But that was where it surely ends

Because, as I have previously mentioned
This was a secret well-intentioned

But somehow those in the know expanded
And as I relate this to you I am trying to be evenhanded

I say this because Grandma, who was much older
Knew all about it, though no one would admit to having
told her

So by now the circle of those with title of "insider"
Had grown quite a bit and indeed was much wider

Those who told me I cannot recall
It was more than one but less than all

Each time I was admonished not to tell a soul
For strict confidentiality was the goal

I said not a word but found it so funny
That I admit I finally told my honey

She laughed because she already knew
And I found myself chagrined too

At last the matter was publicly revealed
And with (feigned?) surprise and delight the whole
family squealed

Winking and nodding without the slightest of guile
There was joy in knowing and all had a smile

In the end, not a single person had been left out
They were all in the know without a doubt

Proud they were of their decorum
They had kept it within such a small forum

After all 'twas a secret it was true
And that meant no one knew

I am proud that this poem got me compared to Ogden Nash by a friend. It is a pretty good poem if I dare say so myself.

The inspiration is of course yet another true story. One of my cousins was pregnant and wanted to keep it a secret. This is what actually happened.

We are wonderful family, but perhaps not the best at secrecy.

WHO'S TALKING?

I think I elevated you a notch
I thought about it as I was drinking scotch

You're amazing, handsome, sweet, and kind
And your views and mine are completely aligned

Your wonderfulness is plain to see
I'm guessing you think the same of me

So, now, don't look surprised and gawking
Maybe it's just the scotch that's talking

Or maybe, just maybe, what I say is true
We'll know in the morning when we'll see what's new

Yikes—another scotch poem! Say it ain't so. But here it is. I guess it is pretty self-explanatory.

WISDOM IS LOOKING DEEPER

If you look for trouble in a man—you will certainly find it

But if you look for good things in the same man—you will (likely) find that, too

God's mystery is that when you strip away the shell, we have kernels both savory and rotten

When we reproach the faults of others, are we beyond reproach ourselves—have we no bitter kernels?

A wise person is aware of the rotten kernels in another person but minds but little, so enamored is he with the taste of what is savory in that person

This poem is self-explanatory and also doesn't rhyme

My wife taught me to live this way and I do my best to do exactly this.

Also, this is a major theme in my friendship book. That if you are only willing to be friends with perfect people you will be lonely, which is no fun at all. My friend may not be perfect but, I got news for myself—I'm not perfect either!

BEACH POEM

I went to the beach just to hang out
A whole bunch of fisherman were all about

Each had his pole and his rod and his reel
Plus a bucket with ice instead of a creel

They were all there to fish with one common goal
That's what they do and that's how they roll

It made sense to me—at least at first
But then I noticed they were widely dispersed

Fifty yards or more betwixt their stations
Clearly too far to permit conversations

Seems to me that these guys all got their druthers
From being alone and far away from the others

I would think if I were out there fishing
For a friend to talk to I would be wishing

What would occur if I should conquer my fear
And say to one at day's end, "Join me for a beer?"

Are they alone because they're afraid to connect
Or something much deeper, solitude to dissect?

I won't find the answer in my beach chair I think
So—"Hey—Mr. Fisherman, how 'bout that drink?"

This struck me when I was sitting at the beach. Why do the fishermen sit so far from each other? I mean it is kind of lonely and boring. Wouldn't they want to hang out with each other? Maybe it's because we men have so much trouble making friends. Anyway, this is what I thought about at the time.

If you are wondering, I chickened out from asking the fisherman to have a drink, which I still regret, as a road not taken.

PIG POEM

Schweinchen was a little pig
She ran around, she danced a jig

The men all thought she was a hottie
And a black belt in karate

But then, when all was said and done
She was my wife, my heart, my sun

I am not sure I should put this in a book, but here goes.

My wife and I have a strong focus on pigs. For some reason, we have gone hog-wild and have a house with over a thousand pigs in it—not live ones, if you are wondering. Even the front yard has eleven pig topiaries.

Getting crazier, my wife's affectionate nickname is Sweetie Pig. And for the coup de grâce, I write her various pig poems. This is one inspired by a German friend who told me how to say "little pig" in German.

Now you really do know everything.

DEATH POEMS

This is odd, even for me. For some reason, on a family vacation, I came up with the idea that we should all write a Death Poem. Sort of like the haiku a Japanese warrior writes before he goes off to die in battle. The family complied, and these poems resulted. I obtained everyone's permission to include them in my book. They are pretty darned good—at least the ones written by other family members are.

And sorry to hog the stage, but I wrote four death poems. I was waiting for them to show up for dinner and had a fair amount of extra time to write the extra poems.

ANDREW CLAYBURN DEATH POEM

What's the point?
Another day of acting
Another day of joy enacting
Yet the struggle is the same
What's the point?

Another person's needs
Another person whom to please
And the trauma is to blame
What's the point?

Another emptiness inside
Another piece of me withers and dies
But this here, this is life
What's the point?

Another soulless smile
Another agonizing uphill mile
I pray for the end of this incessant trial
I mean, What's the point?

BETHANY STACHENFELD DEATH POEM

I'm sitting here, eating ham
Wondering who I am
A wife, a daughter, a CEO—
Just depends who wants to know
Always labeled in the eyes of others
But where does that leave me, when I'm down under?
Buried below six feet of earth
In a casket, that's sealed for sure
I'll leave behind nothing but my impressions
The mark I left on those still standing
I hope people think on me and smile
With memories of fun, love, and beguile
It shouldn't all be light and fond—
I'll have touched on something strong
Sparked some creativity and boldness
Forced friends to break confines that hold them
And pushed to boundaries way past the norm
To do the things that unconform
That will be my legacy
Not money or fame, but how to be

ANN STACHENFELD DEATH POEM

My heart is weary, I have to rest
Don't get teary, and look to the west

The sun setting after shining bright
Will it be today, is this the night?

My life is full, I've done it all
Had true love, beloved children, and broke through the wall

I'll see Kona, Mom, and Dad
There is peace and I'm not sad

Farewell to all I love, the grandbabies I will not see
Long life is impossible and I must flee

KIMBERLY STACHENFELD DEATH POEM

Undone

Death marks the moment where time reverses
A singular moment the hourglass curses

The moment I heard, the moment that last
I looked up her happy mask
Burst into my mind, unsolicited, unasked

And then unspooled our time together
Our hard conversations, softening like old leather

Into the giddiness of early friends
Enjoying good times, unaware of grim ends

Like water draining from the bath
Memories poured forth, with joy and wrath

As my brain removed her from its support
And built from friends still breathing, a new fort

MY DEATH POEM #1

Sorry if this sounds too cynical
But I've now reached life's pinnacle
I've time and money with which to frolic
But I'm not an alcoholic
I'm kind of noisy and not quiet
And I'm also on a low-salt diet
Pretty girls are such a treat
But on my wife, I never cheat
I'm quite proud of what I've done
But I know that Luck has caused my run
I have family and friends
For the joy that it sends
I am finally alive
At age 65
Now I ask why
Is it time to die?

MY DEATH POEM #2

What's it all about? I sat and wondered
As outside the lightning storm thundered

Could it be that my life has meaning
Or is it all just dreaming seeming?

My mood of late's gone to one of gloom
Feels so much like coming doom

Maybe nothing means anything at all
Nothing more than the outside storm's squall

If this is so then nothing matters
We can be super cool or mad as hatters

If I take this to its obvious conclusion
All there is is complete illusion

Alas, I say, I'm giving up the ghost
To the end of life this is my toast

MY DEATH POEM #3

The end, the end, the end is near
I say to my buddy as I drink my beer

He acknowledges me with a sidelong glance
As each day it's my usual dance

"But tonight is different," I say with steam
Even though it might not so seem

The fever's burning in my eyes
He looks at me with real surprise

"Are you okay? I'm really worried"
My actions are just a bit too hurried

"Perhaps we should talk," he says direct
My emotional health he must protect

Now he asks earnestly what I have to say
"Ah, never mind, same shit, different day"

MY DEATH POEM #4

How then should I die?
Should I go peacefully and content my life was well lived
Or rage against the dying of the light, like that immortal poem?
Or say good-bye to all and sundry with my sage advice?
In my will shall I give instructions to be carefully followed?
Should I write my own obituary?
Should I forgive all those who transgressed against me?
Perhaps I should die in a battle achieving a worthy cause
Or maybe just relax calmly and let death come to me as it comes to all

www.ingramcontent.com/pod-product-compliance
Lightning Source LLC
Chambersburg PA
CBHW030248160726
48262CB00001B/5

* 9 7 8 1 6 3 2 2 6 1 7 7 9 *